Online Dating: Avoid The Catfish!

(How To Date Online Successfully)

Kevin Darné

About the Author

Kevin Darné is the President & CEO of Conation Enterprises, a company dedicated to helping people facilitate change within; in order to bring about change without. Kevin is also the author of My Cat Won't Bark! (A Relationship Epiphany). The book is about learning how to approach relationships with complete awareness, having realistic expectations, and using self-empowerment techniques. My Cat Won't Bark! is laced with several humorous anecdotes and has received noteworthy positive editorial reviews from the likes of Publishers Weekly, Reader's Favorite, and Midwest Book Review.

Kevin's insight into the tricky world of dating, has been featured on WGN-TV Morning News Chicago, The Chicago Tribune, NBCNews.com, Askmen.com, ReadersDigest.com, Bravotv.com, HowStuffWorks.com, PsychologyToday.com, Bustle.com, Thisisinsider.com, Stylecaster.com, Match.com, Cheatsheet.com, Babble.com, Romper.com, Zoosk.com, Tinder, AARP.org, Redbookmag.com, and several other digital publications and radio appearances.

For additional information visit http://lovealert911.com/

Reviving Hearts with Awareness & Self-Empowerment

"Never love anyone who treats you like you're ordinary." – Oscar Wilde

Avoid the Catfish! goes against the conventional wisdom of today's dating scene, whereby everyone seems to be interested in speeding things up. According to a Pew Research Center poll conducted in 2016, approximately 15% of U.S. adults have used an online dating site or app. Some people spend hours each day swiping left and right, as they scan through profiles of potential dating matches. If there is a mutual interest, the two people set up a time to meet.

GPS-based dating apps allow people to connect with each other based upon where they are presently located at any given moment. If two people happen to be at the same concert, nightclub, or shopping mall, they can arrange to meet for a drink right away.

In large metropolitan areas, speed dating is another option for quickly meeting new people to potentially date. One example is Chicago First Dates. This company, and others like it, host events at various locations a few times each month. On average, they charge $35 per person and the rules vary depending on the event and the age group being targeted.

One example of such an event had rules whereby women remained seated at a table and men switched tables every five minutes. According to the advertisement on the company website, each person is promised to have up to ten chats with potential love interests. The day after the event, the company informs you of any matches. These are prospects who mutually chose each other.

Facebook announced plans to offer Facebook Dating in 2018. The initial roll out took place in Columbia and is expected to go worldwide eventually. However, there has been speculation that Facebook's ulterior motive is to retain youthful users who have gradually reduced the amount of time they spend on Facebook. Only time will tell if the objective is to create an atmosphere for people to find a love connection or simply to increase opportunities for advertisers to sell their products and services to users. One advantage Facebook has is it has almost two billion users!

Whether one elects to use online dating sites, apps, speed dating events, or social media, the emphasis is clearly on generating a large pool of options and having the ability to quickly engage. There is a tendency for people to go out on dates without having established much rapport in advance. This is likely to increase their number of bad or awkward first dates. Experiencing too many bad first dates can lead to dating burnout, cynicism, and in some instances cause people to give up on finding a suitable partner altogether.

If you want something different, *you* have to do something different. When it comes to choosing dating prospects, it might be wise to adhere to the old proverb: "Measure twice, cut once."

Contents

Introduction	1
Six Mistakes People Make	11
Frustration: When Reality Smacks Expectation	19
You Attract What You Are Ready For	27
Look Before You Leap	33
Let's Get Started	39
Avoid the Catfish!	49
Sidestep the Long-Distance Trap	59
Dodge the Friend Zone	65
Relax and Have Fun!	73
Parting Thoughts	81
Additional Resources	85

Introduction

We live in an era where meeting and dating available singles has changed dramatically from years gone by. Long before there was online dating, we had "computer dating" whose invention has been credited to two Harvard students in 1965. Their names are Jeff Tarr and Vaugh Morrill. Dave Crump and Doug Ginsberg are also noted for contributing to *Operation Match*.

Unlike most online dating sites and apps today where everyone can create and search profiles of other people they're interested in, *Operation Match* was designed to match your interest and desires to another person who was in the system, by having them answer a series of questions. Punch cards were produced and fed into a room size computer. It took up to six weeks to have your matches mailed to you for the price of three dollars and the cost of a stamp. Essentially, it was a high-tech blind date venture.

By the time *Operation Match* was sold in 1968, it is estimated they had solicited one million respondents and some of them actually got married. They attributed this to odds rather than any scientific input. Today we still see elements of *Operation Match* in online dating sites such as eHarmony, where members are required to answer a detailed 400 question survey in order to be matched up with suitable prospects. Initially, the emphasis is on compatibility not chemistry. Regardless of which online dating site or app that is used, there are pluses and minuses.

Advantages of Online Dating

You can be proactive when it comes to seeking a mate or companion.

There is a built-in buffer zone between you and those you meet.

You have the opportunity to meet people you otherwise would not have met anywhere else.

Theoretically, those online are in the market to meet and date new people.

You can make contact without seeming too aggressive or desperate.

You have a huge pool of prospects to choose from and weigh your options.

You have time to craft your image the way you want to present yourself.

Your profile works for you 24/7 unless you choose to hide or make it inactive.

Within your profile, you can openly state what you are looking for in a mate.

You control if and when you will exchange contact information or meet someone in person.

Disadvantages of Online Dating

You don't know if there is *real chemistry* between you and them if it's strictly online.

You can't always rely on photos or information provided in profiles as being accurate.

Your writing style or grammar may not present you at your best.

You may become addicted to interacting with people online and never take things offline.

Some people misrepresent themselves for fun or to scam and use others.

The vast majority of online dating services allow members to freely interact with one another, after they have established profiles and paid access/membership fees. It is up to you the member to do your own screening and selecting. Too often, people tend to forget it was *them* who *selected* their date or chose to engage with whomever.

Online dating sites are nothing more than a *tool for meeting new people*. Much like a fork is a tool for eating. You can use it to eat a garden salad or a slice of double fudge chocolate cake. However, no obese person would ever blame their fork for their weight gain! And yet, people who have bad dating experiences with those they met online will blame the whole online dating industry. Just remember, each of us *chooses* our own friends, lovers, and spouses!

Do you take responsibility for *your* choices and decisions in life?

If so, you are in the vanishing minority. Not long ago I published the following article.

Online Dating: Is Everyone a Catfish, Conman, Liar, Cheater, Predator or Loser?

Every other week, it seems we learn about nightmare experiences people have had with online dating. Whether it's a conman like Ray Holycross/*The Internet Casanova* using various aliases to scam 38 women in seven states; Ronaiah Tuiasosopo, a *catfish* guy, creating a fake Internet profile pretending to be a woman causing Manti Teo the Notre Dame football player to emotionally invest in a non-existent relationship, or others who were attacked or killed by a person they met online. The message for many people is: Only a fool would try online dating!

Facts and Stats

First and foremost, it is important to remember that media outlets, newspapers, and magazines are in business to make a profit. Secondly horror stories and articles that elicit our fears sell very well. Statisticbrain.

com put together the following online dating data back in June 2012.

Total number of single people in the United States – 54 Million

The total number of people in the United States who have tried online dating – 40 Million

Total eHarmony members – 20 Million

Total Match.com members – 15 Million

Average length of courtship *before marriage* for those who met online – 18.5 months

Average length of courtship *before marriage* for those who met offline – 42 months

Percent of *all sex offenders* who choose to use online dating sites to meet people -10%

Men lie mostly about: Age, height, and income.

Women lie mostly about: Weight, physical build, and age.

These statistics aren't likely to sell a lot of newspapers or generate website clicks. Interestingly, people who met online got married much sooner than those who met offline. A few years ago, a major online dating site touted 1 in 5 couples who get married met online. However, before anyone gets too excited, it's the same as saying 80% of couples who marry met offline!

Truth be told, whether you meet someone online or offline odds are, you're probably not going to end up marrying them. When it comes to love and relationships, most of us *fail our way* to success. If this were not true, we would all be married to our high school sweethearts!

Whatever traits you believed made for an *ideal mate* at age 17, 20, or 22, are not likely to be the same traits you value at age 25, 30, or beyond. Our *must haves* list evolves with life experiences.

Keep Things in Perspective

Whenever you say, "There aren't any *quality people* online," you should keep in mind; other people are saying the exact same thing, despite the fact *you* have an online profile!

The same people that are online go to the grocery store, movie theatre, beach, park, nightclubs, shopping malls, and church. It's not *where* you meet but *whom* you meet that counts!

The Internet did not invent liars and cheaters. It's important to use good commonsense when dealing with strangers, whether you met them online or offline.

Anything Worthwhile is Rarely Free

Avoid free or super cheap dating websites; they tend to attract the *shadiest* people. I know there are always going to be *exceptions*. My guess is, somewhere in Chicago, there is a dumpster which contains a diamond ring. However, if I were shopping for such a ring, I would choose to visit a jewelry store or other places *known* for selling quality diamond rings over dumpster diving.

Selecting a *free* online site is like moving into an economically depressed section of town and complaining about the high crime rate. If you know what type of person you're looking for, your next step is to find out which sites *they* are likely to join. There are also numerous *niche* online dating sites geared towards a particular age, race, religion, sexual orientation, and other demographics. Research pays dividends. Be selective!

After I gave this advice to one woman she said, "I don't feel like I should have to pay for love." Becoming a member of an online dating site is no more paying to find love than it would be to pay a cover charge to get into a nightclub.

Both the online dating membership fee and the cover charge merely *grants you access* to other people who are there. You're simply *joining the party*. Some people are hoping to connect with a special someone and others are looking for casual dating, intimate encounters, or finding chat buddies. Online dating sites are like virtual nightclubs without the alcohol and crowded dance floors. You still have to introduce yourself and conduct your own screening process.

A profile serves one of two purposes. If it's yours, it's a "Help wanted ad" and if it's another person's, "it's a resume". In the business world most companies take their time and interview several candidates as well as do background checks on those they are *seriously considering* before making a job offer. At the end of the day *you* are responsible for *your* choices in life.

Forget the mistake.
Remember the lesson.

Six Mistakes People Make

Selecting Without Researching

There are lots of new online dating websites popping up every day. One very common mistake people often make is assuming they are all about the same. Intellectually, you know that can't be true. Would anyone compare staying at Motel 6 to staying at The Ritz Carlton or Four Seasons Hotel by simply noting they all have beds and cable television? Do you believe a steak dinner at Denny's is just as good as one at Ruth Chris Steakhouse or Morton's Steakhouse? No!

Yet, when it comes to online dating sites many people do not exercise discriminating taste when making a site selection. You owe it to yourself to at least do a few Google searches to view the best or top-rated dating sites. Also, be aware there are sites that cater to particular interests. Before you sign up with any site, you should ask yourself: If I were *my* "Mr. Right" or "Ms. Right" which online dating site or app would I choose?

Bad Profile Photo

Another big mistake is using a horrible profile photo! Examples include those who stand in front of a bathroom mirror holding a cell phone or pictures taken overhead with the subject looking up. Attempting to hide body size, photos holding a dog, cat, or some other pet, photos showing your exe's hand resting on your shoulder even though you have cropped his or her face out, glamour shots, zany or stupid facial expressions, those taken standing next to your best friend who by the way may be more attractive than you in the viewer's eyes: are bad. A profile photo is your calling card and the viewer's focus should only be on you. There's enough competition already on the site.

Lying

Lying about age, weight, career, and relationship status is a mistake. Eventually the truth comes out! Now to be fair, some of these websites make it easy to be evasive with such options as "I'd rather not say" or "I'll tell you later". You can have a relationship status listing "it's complicated" or a body type listing "a *few* pounds to lose". If one has to be discreet, they are involved with someone. Anyone with thirty pounds to lose is kidding them self by calling that a "few". If someone were hitting you on the head 30 times, you wouldn't call that a few.

Asking for the World!

"Don't expect to sit next to the moon unless you are a star!" Too many people are unrealistic when it comes to their search for a mate. They create a long list of requirements or traits that even they do not possess themselves. It is just as important to illustrate what makes *you* special. Like attracts like. Others take the opposite approach and list everything they do not want. (No players, no liars, no cheaters, no games, etc.) Without realizing it, they are announcing to the world this is who they have chosen in past relationships. It also comes across as if you are negative, bitter, or have a chip on your shoulder. Does anyone really believe a player who is attracted to you is not going to contact you simply because you said you do not want to deal with players? It should go without saying if a trait is not on your list of wants, then it is not something you desire. Focusing on the negative is never attractive. For those who may require help creating a profile there are services such as Profilehelper.com which offer online dating profile services.

Meeting too Quickly

Another very common mistake is exchanging personal contact information and setting up dates too quickly. One of the great things about online dating websites is that you can get a feel for someone by how well they communicate with you through the site. You can use the online service's instant messaging to chat as well as email one another through the site. If a man or woman starts to rush you into meeting with him or her, more often than not, it is because he or she is afraid they may expose some character flaw that might deter you.

Some women are afraid of becoming too emotionally invested with someone they have yet to meet. This forces them to hurry with exchanging contact information and meeting a guy too quickly. Hopefully you are communicating with multiple prospects and evaluating your options based upon the responses you get to questions you ask, their sense of humor, and things you have in common. You are responsible for your choices.

Pushing for Exclusive Status too Quickly

Lots of women are in a hurry to tie down a relationship with someone they barely know! The whole purpose of casual dating is to *determine* if this person is someone you want to have a serious relationship with. Casual dating does not mean having sex with everyone you have dinner with. It means taking things one step at a time and allowing them to unfold naturally. Dating is an exploratory process, so it's often counterproductive to state on your profile that you're looking for a serious relationship, a marriage-minded person, or God-fearing man.

Anyone who proclaims they are *ready to get married* and they do not have a boyfriend or girlfriend is someone who is putting the cart before the horse. Ideally, your special significant other should be the impetus for why you are suddenly having thoughts of marriage. Otherwise you are just someone who is chasing after a marital status and needs a *prop* to succeed.

Attempting to jump into a one-on-one dating situation right off the bat, is like job hunting by sending out one resume at a time and waiting to see if that company will interview you and eventually hire you before you send out another resume to a different company. Realistically, you can't determine if he or she is "the one" until after you get to know each other better and that takes time. Be yourself and encourage him or her to do the same. No one goes to a buffet and stops only at the first station. The vast majority of people walk around and check out all the stations before deciding upon what they will eat. Every serious relationship I have ever had, began casually and *evolved* into something serious.

It's also a mistake to automatically assume that just because someone has gone out with you a couple of times they should take down their profile. Unless you have agreed to be exclusive, you both should keep your options open. Trying to skip the dating process in order to get married, can lead to regret. *Dating is not a waste of time. Being married to the wrong person is.*

Frustration **always comes** before **achievement**

Frustration: When Reality Smacks Expectation

An article was recently published by someone who was frustrated with the online dating process. As I read it, I began to realize there are probably many people who feel the same way as that writer did. The following is my response to his list of six complaints.

Most of the Member Profiles Are Inactive

Life is all about timing. Just because someone we are interested in is either no longer on the market or has decided to focus on another method to meet people doesn't mean online dating sites are a scam. To be honest with you, it is up to the individual to delete their account!

Maybe the member has not deleted their account because they may want to come back at some point. Either way, this is not the fault of the dating site!

There Are Sketchy People Out There

This is true, but these same people are also at the grocery store, nightclubs, malls, restaurants, parks, beaches, university campuses, and even churches. Online dating sites did not invent "sketchy people"! Naturally, one should use good commonsense when it comes to meeting strangers. It is up to you to have your own mate selection/screening process and *must haves* list.

The Person You Meet May Not Be the Person You Were Corresponding With

Yes, there are some people who set up fake profiles, use other people's photos, and lie about all sorts of things. This is a very small percentage of people. Most members are not inclined to spend money joining online dating sites as a catfish. Granted, there are some con artists who are seeking financial gains by tugging at one's heartstrings. However, with some caution and a little effort, it is not difficult to uncover the truth or at the very least spot *red flags*.

Online Dating Makes You Shallow

Most people spend time with those they are *attracted to* and whose company they enjoy. Men in particular, rarely ask someone out whom they are *not attracted* to. Everyone has *their* list of requirements as well as preferences. As the old adage goes: "Beauty is in the eye of the beholder." Thankfully, not everyone is attracted to the same type of people.

A fear of missing out is more likely to be a challenge rather than being shallow. Having a large pool of people to potentially connect with can cause some individuals to become *shopaholics*. Searching through profiles and connecting with others via the site is what gives them a high. Meeting *in person* or finding someone for an exclusive relationship is no longer their priority.

Online Dating Warps Your Sense of Intimacy

This one has some validity with regard to having felt like you've known someone longer because of your online communication time. You might not ordinarily have sex with someone you just met. However, if you have been communicating with someone for a few weeks via online, phone conversations, email, and texts prior to meeting in person, I suspect this would cause you to feel more comfortable on a first date than you otherwise would had you met only offline.

Having established a good rapport prior to meeting someone, eliminates a lot of the first date jitters. It is also easy for some people to forget this is a *first* date because an emotional connection was formed prior to them meeting. This happens with *Pen Pals* as well.

There is no asterisk or special credit given just because you have been in contact for weeks or months prior to meeting in person. It's still having sex on the *first* date. Nevertheless, having sex is a *choice* and each person is entitled to have their own criteria as to when to say, "yes".

Couples in long distance relationships are also prone to counting *calendar time* as being the same as *actual time they have been together.* A person who is dating someone locally and has only seen their mate ten times in person thus far, is not likely to have thoughts of marriage.

However, the same people in a long-distance relationship who have been corresponding via email, phone, text, Skype, and social media for a year, might decide to become engaged even though they too have only been together *in person* ten times or less! They will also state they have been a couple for a year even though their *actual time together* is less than two weeks. Emotional connections transcend time and the normal dating courtship protocol.

Race Relations Are Horrible in Online Dating Sites

Race relations are no more horrible than they are offline. People are more likely to reveal their *true nature* online. Not long-ago, YouTube had to remove the comments section from a Cheerios commercial that featured an interracial married couple who had a bi-racial daughter. She lovingly placed Cheerios on her black father's heart while he is sleeping so he'd be healthy. Naturally, behind the mask of anonymity racist comments were posted. As was mentioned previously, the Internet and online dating sites did not create these people.

Fortunately, there are niche online dating sites available for those who may be seeking to date people from different races, religions, and cultures. Rejection is always going to be a possibility whether it is due to someone's race, weight, height, hair or lack of, smoker versus non-smoker, or drinker versus non-drinker. When it is all said and done, *no* is still *no* regardless of the reason.

Strange Irony

The writer of the original article that complained about online dating admitted he met his girlfriend online! That is the equivalent of saying; "I hate online dating, but it works!"

"**A Kiss** that is never tasted, is **forever and ever** wasted." – Billie Holiday

You Attract What You Are Ready For

Are you ready to date? I realize this may sound like a silly question given you purchased an online dating book. However, you would be surprised at how many people I speak with who want a mate but *hate* the dating process. The fact of the matter is, your subconscious mind will never allow you to succeed at anything you despise! Your attitude affects your altitude.

Dating is supposed to be a fun sociable activity. If your mindset is not in a place where you want to get to know new people and embrace new experiences, then you are probably not ready to date at this point. Having a negative or unenthusiastic approach towards the dating process is the stink of death! People can pick up on your vibe without you expressing your thoughts, simply by observing your tone and posture. No one wants to be around a cynical or standoffish person.

If you just got out of a relationship, think all men are no good cheating dogs, or believe all women are gold diggers looking for a meal ticket, then you are not in the right frame of mind to be meeting new people! If you're looking to date in order to pass the time while secretly hoping to get back with your ex or you really are unsure of what you want to get out of the dating process then you are not ready. It's important to *know yourself, love yourself,* and *trust yourself* before pursing dating and relationships. This requires taking the time to do some serious introspective thinking with regard to your past mate selection choices. It's important to rid ourselves of any *emotional baggage* we have been carrying around from past relationships.

Being honest with oneself is the first step towards finding happiness, not only with a future mate but with life in general. If you have no real interest in dating or being in a relationship, making half-hearted measures will only cause you to become more cynical.

There is nothing wrong with being single and free. It's not necessary to be dating, in an exclusive relationship, or married, in order to live a happy and fulfilling life! Too often, people fall prey to peer pressure from friends, family, or others who feel sorry for those without a mate. This may cause a person to join an online dating site or take steps to find a mate just to fit in.

Life is a *personal* journey! You are responsible for your own happiness. You have to know what you want to be happy. The world may not owe you anything but *you* owe yourself the world!

At this point, if you have decided that maybe you're not truly ready to date I highly recommend you purchase *My Cat Won't Bark! (A Relationship Epiphany).* The reader is encouraged to take an inward journey, to examine their past relationship choices and to take those lessons they have learned and apply them. The book also dispels many commonly held myths regarding dating and relationships.

Knowing what you want should **determine where** you shop…

Look Before You Leap

We live in an era where when it comes to choosing a restaurant, a book, a movie, or to purchase most consumer products, the majority of us will spend some time researching and reading reviews before we decide to invest our money. Yet the approach most people take with online dating is they will simply choose a site, any site.

In some instances, people choose a site based upon name awareness or the price of the monthly membership. They do not stop to put themselves in the shoes of the type of person they want to meet and then ask themselves if such a person would most likely sign up on Tinder, OkCupid, Match.com, Plenty of Fish, Zoosk, eHarmony, OurTime, Christian Mingle, EliteSingles or so on.

If you know what type of person you want to meet, you can narrow down the possible sites and apps for you to consider. There are companies who specialize in reviewing dating websites and apps. Some of them breakdown sites by their ease of use, functionality, average educational and income level, race, religion, gender ratio, age, sexual orientation, and other demographics. Accumulating some granular details regarding dating sites and apps in addition to simply finding out how many members, their popularity, and monthly fees, can save you time in the long run.

Among the sites you may want to search for target demographics, reviews, and comparisons are www.datingadvice.com, www.datingscout.com, and www.datingsitesreviews.com. However, before you accept any of these online dating site reviewers as being completely impartial, it would not surprise me if some of them are being compensated to receive higher rankings. Nevertheless, getting some basic facts about these dating sites at *no charge* is worth your time. In addition to providing reviews, many of these sites provide inciteful articles with dating advice.

Niche Sites for Those with Serious Must Haves

In addition to the most popular online dating websites and apps, there are also niche sites for those who have strict *must have* requirements. These may range from particular hobbies, interests, or other things one wants with regard to compatibility in someone they choose to date. A few examples are SingleParentMeet.com, FitnessSingles.com, BikerPlanet.com, Farmersonly.com, GamerDating.com, PetPeopleMeet.com, RepublicanPeopleMeet.com, and DemocratPeoplemeet.com. For just about every potential "must have" requirement one may have, there is a bound to be a niche dating site. Unfortunately, the disadvantage is, most likely there will be fewer options for you to choose from as these sites are likely to have fewer members. However, if something is extremely important to you, it may be worth it to choose a niche site.

For those looking for casual encounters there are hookup sites such as BeNaughty.com, Xmatch.com, AdultFriendfinder.com, Grindr.com, Passion.com, and Lucky App. Some hookup sites are known to have several fake profiles to lure men, along with escorts looking to earn cash.

"Every **Journey** Begins with a **Single Step.**"
– Mya Angelou

Let's Get Started

Create a New Email Account

Before we venture into the sea of online dating, there are some prerequisites. The first step is to set up an email account specifically for your online dating adventures. You may choose Yahoo, Gmail, AOL, MSN, or whatever you prefer. However, the most important thing you want to do when setting up the account is avoid using any part of your name. For example, if you were signing up for a Yahoo account where it asks you for your first and last name, you could enter your first name as Wonderful and your last name as Lady. Your email would appear as <u>wonderfullady@yahoo.com</u> or you might use Happy for your first name and Guy for your last name which would appear as <u>happyguy@yahoo.com</u>. The purpose of doing this is for safety and privacy reasons. An email that provides your actual first and last name, could give anyone enough information to start researching you and your possible whereabouts.

You do not want to reveal too much about yourself until you feel comfortable with someone. Practically every other day we hear or see stories in the news about stalkers. The last thing you want is some stranger showing up at your door without having established a rapport with you. Eventually, you will find yourself exchanging personal email addresses after you have been communicating for a while using the dating site's instant messaging tool. Having an email address which retains your anonymity allows you to maintain control of the pace at which people will learn more about you. Some people start off by only revealing their first name.

Purchase a Visa or American Express Gift Card

In the event you have chosen an online dating site which requires a credit card to pay a monthly, quarterly, semi-annual, or annual fee, it would be best to use a gift card instead of one of your actual credit cards. Several online dating sites are notorious for conducting *automatic renewals*.

To avoid the hassle of trying to get them to credit back your credit card, use a gift card instead and make sure you spend any remaining money you have on it after you have been initially billed by the dating site. I would advise you to prepay for three months minimum and six months maximum. In all honesty, if you haven't had any dating success within the first three months you may want to consider moving to another site or app. On the other hand, you may get lucky very early on and in both of these scenarios if you have prepaid for several months in advance you may find yourself stuck with a paid profile. Inactive profiles can be explained by the fact that members move on to other sites, found love, or simply gave up looking. One of the worst surprises in the world is to later discover your credit card has been charged for a renewal. Naturally, if you are having a blast using the dating site you may want to use your credit card for future renewals.

Get a Phone Number from Google Voice

Google Voice is a free service and provides phone numbers which can be accessed through your computer and if you download the app you can use it on your smartphone. The service provides you with a phone number to reach you which is not your personal number and is free within the U.S. You can also have calls made to that number forwarded to any phone you desire. For additional information visit https://voice.google.com/about. You may also find the following YouTube video useful in explaining how to use it: Google Voice Tutorial 2019. .

Creating an Experimental Profile for Observation Purposes

Although I do not advise you to use free online dating sites for the purpose of finding your *ideal mate,* they are a good way to *explore online dating* without having to invest money and they provide a way to learn a few things.

Please create a profile on one of the following free dating sites: https://www.okcupid.com/ https://

datehookup.dating/, http://www.pof.com/ , https://free-datehookup.com/ or any other site which allows searches of member profiles without having to pay.

Just as was suggested with creating your email account, you do not want to use any part of your actual name when creating your online "user name" on the dating website. However, keep in mind whatever user name you go with will be permanent for that dating website. Therefore, the user name you choose should be carefully thought out in the event you end up continuing to use the site. Your user name is part of the first impression others will observe about you. User names such as Hornyguy, SexyLady, or HotNready, pretty much state why a person may be on the site. You probably will also want to avoid names like Waiting4myprince or Desperate4Love. Happy2BMe or Lovinglife are examples of user names that speak towards a person's outlook on life. Some people use their hobby or interest; GardenLady, Boatman, IslandGirl, or MusicMan.

Note: In my opinion, free sites are better off viewed as practice dating sites. Wherever anything is *free,* odds increase; you will have to sift through a lot more riffraff in order to find a jewel.

Search Through Profiles

Most dating sites are fairly self-explanatory. They will ask you to input your gender, the gender you're seeking, an age range, body type, and the amount of distance from your zip code you will consider a possibility. Some sites get even more granular where they ask you to select what type of relationship you are looking for as in serious relationship, casual dating, friendship, or an intimate encounter. I have also seen some dating sites that allow you to specify habits or vices such as smoker, non-smoker, drinker, non-drinker, along with children or no children. Current relationship or marital status, race, religion, body type, education, and income, are also fairly common filters available for narrowing down a search.

During this exercise, I want you to read through several profiles of both genders. It can't hurt to see how your competition is presenting themselves. I suspect you will see a lot of cell phone selfies used as either profile photos or as part of an album. Some of the worst are those taken in front of a bathroom mirror. There will also be some fairly tasteless ones that focus on aspects of one's anatomy. These may include shirtless men showing off a six pack, a bulge in their pants or shorts, women with a tight shot of their cleavage or posing sideways to display the size and roundness of their behinds. Anyone blatantly presenting their image as body parts, should not be surprised by the *quality* of their contacts. Having said that, if one is strictly looking to just get laid then those types of photos are likely to work like magic. The real challenge comes when you reach out to others that you are attracted to for a possible meaningful relationship. They may be turned off by your photos or even offended *you* contacted them!

Profile Summaries

You will most likely see some people who barely list anything about themselves. They could be simply checking out the website like you are doing. It is also possible they are just plain lazy and lack communication skills. This is especially so if they also barely state what they are looking for. You will probably see many half-hearted profiles that begin with: "I never thought I'd be doing this..." Or "A friend of mine found the love of her life online so I thought I'd give it shot. If you like what you see hit me up and we'll see where things take us." Or "It's me again, I thought I would give *this* another shot." Or "My friends dared me to create a profile. Here I am!"

People who present themselves too casually or laid back in their profile search for a mate, are probably not going to put much effort into a relationship either. A certain amount of enthusiasm or positivity is required to attract most people. You will also want to beware of jokester profiles. These people attempt to overcompensate with humor in order to hide their insecurities. Unless one is a standup comedian by trade, you are better off not attempting to blast away on every line, especially if you believe sarcasm is a *people magnet* because it is not.

Too much information is another profile type to watch out for. These people list every good or bad experience they have ever had and then proceed to not only list what they are looking for but also what they are not looking for. Very often, they come off as being cynical, demanding, or simply looking for something which does not exist; such as perfection.

Creating a Winning Profile

Your profile is equivalent to being a resume and a wanted ad. It is a marketing tool. The goal is twofold in that you want to present yourself as being a catch and also reveal what you are looking for as well. Generally speaking, profiles which contain a photo get more views than those without. If you doubt this, note how often *you* bother to read profiles without photos.

Photo

If at all possible, use a photo where you are the only person featured. Make sure your face is clearly visible. Avoid any zany looks or facial expressions. If you want to display that side of your personality you can add them to your album page which shows additional photos. Try not to use any photos which would give too much information about your exact location, cars with your license plate displayed or ones which feature your home street address and so on. It is perfectly acceptable to just have your headshot photo on the dating site or app.

A Description of Who You Are

Most sites will contain an area to display some information about yourself and things you enjoy doing. This is also the area where it is common to mention a few "bucket list" goals you would like to try to achieve some day or places you would like to visit. Try not to put so much here that you do not have anything new to say about yourself later when you are corresponding.

State What You Are Looking For

This is the section where people often unintentionally come off sounding negative. They list all of their *deal breakers* as opposed to traits they are *looking for*. There are ways to express them without sounding negative.

Instead of saying; No Liars! No Cheaters! No Players! You might want to say something along the lines of: "I am an honest and straightforward person and would appreciate those same qualities in my mate." Your goal is to clearly state the traits you *want* in your ideal mate.

Yeah, I think **I'm going** to go ahead and **pass on** that…

Avoid the Catfish!

Catfish: The TV Show premiered on MTV in November 2012. The show revealed some truths and lies about online dating. It was created after a documentary film had been made about an online dating experience Nev Schulman had, where he learned the person he loved didn't exist.

A "catfish" is someone who creates a fake profile for an online dating or social media site using someone else's photos and a made-up bio profile, for the purpose of tricking someone to fall in love with them. Some victims communicate with their catfish for several months or even years without ever having met in person or doing a live video chat.

The show is typically presented with the victim having contacted the producers because he or she suspects they are being catfished and would like to find out if the person they have fallen in love with really exists and if so why he or she has avoided meeting in person.

According to a 2013 Hollywood.com report, the truth is, most people contacting the show were actually *the catfish*. They generally wanted to come clean because they felt guilty or they hoped once the victim knew the truth, he or she might still accept the *real* them as a potential mate.

The catfish, in some instances, was a person the victim knew. They might even be someone who had been placed in the victim's "friend zone" or a person they casually knew of but had no romantic interest in. More often than not, the catfish was someone who resided a great distance away.

The level of deception can be very extreme with men pretending to be women and vice versa or people who are morbidly obese using the image of a fashion model as their profile photo. Loneliness and fear of rejection is often cited as the initial reason why the person became a catfish. They wanted to create an exciting and romantic life for themselves. Gradually, they found themselves digging a hole in which they did not know how to get out of.

One of the most famous catfish stories involves former Notre Dame football player Manti Te'o who met Lennay Kekua online and fell in love. He revealed to the media she was the love of his life and she had died on the same day he lost his grandmother. It turns out the image of the woman used in the profile was created by a man. The actual woman never heard of Te'o! Ronaiah Tuiasosopo described as a family friend or acquaintance of Te'o confessed to the hoax. He admitted to falling in love with Te'o and using the Kekua identity as an escape. As hurtful as it must be to be catfished, it has to be extremely embarrassing to be a quasi-public figure and have your story make national news.

Things can always go from bad to worse when it comes to being catfished. Some catfish are not out to solely make friends or establish a romantic emotional relationship. Their goal is to find someone they can take advantage of financially. One woman by the name of Sandie, age 63, was a guest on the Dr. Phil talk show. She admitted to sending $63,000 to a man she had never met! She connected with Max on Match.com. According to his profile he was from Texas. Max told Sandie he was in the army working on a top-secret mission in Afghanistan. He proposed to her after only two months of communicating. Every time they were going to meet *something* always got in the way. One time, he supposedly went AWOL but got caught up in a battle with the Taliban and suffered a severe hand wound. Fifty thousand dollars of the sixty-three thousand she sent him, was shipped *inside cereal boxes* to help him get $1 million in gold bars out of customs in Ghana. All of this took place within *six months* of her meeting Max online.

A private investigation firm hired by the Dr. Phil Show, was able to track down the scammer in Nigeria. There were several red flags Sandie overlooked, including Max wearing a Marine uniform in his profile photo while claiming to be in the army, his broken English in phone call conversations and emails, as well as lacking the slightest hint of a Texas accent.

Another woman by the name of LeAnn met a man named Terry on a dating site who told her he was a petroleum engineer from Houston, Texas living in Alaska. Every time they were planning to meet, something always came up. He had to travel to India due to a civil lawsuit. He mentioned in passing, he needed money to pay a judge. LeAnn sent him $3200 but noted Terry never asked her for the money, she *volunteered* it. Stating hardships is a tactic sometimes called *dry* begging. The sympathetic listener offers to help without actually being *asked* to do so.

A woman by the name of Dawn sent a man she met online named David $30,000.

In each and every one of these instances, these women had never actually met the men in person. In a rather short amount of time, they were emotionally invested and sent their hard-earned money and retirement savings to complete strangers. Loneliness and gullibility apparently go hand in hand.

Look for Digital Footprints

Before you seriously start contemplating meeting someone, you owe it to yourself to see what you can uncover about them as well as verify what information they have revealed to you. Naturally, if you are considering sending someone $50,000 in boxes of Cheerios, you probably should run that past a best friend or close family member who loves you.

Initially, you will want to start with doing a Google search of the person's name. If you have copied and saved any photos of the person you have met online, you can also upload them after clicking on the camera icon in Google Search images. This search will provide links to other webpages where the image has been used. You can also use this for photos of buildings as well.

You should conduct searches on some of the most popular social media sites such as Facebook, Instagram, Snapchat, Twitter, LinkedIn, YouTube, and Pinterest. It would be highly unlikely to meet someone in this day and age who does not have at least one of these social media accounts.

There are websites geared towards alerting the public about known scammers, along with images and email addresses they've used. PigBusters.net and Male-Scammers.com are two such sites.

Another source of good information can be found on sites like fastpeoplesearch.com; which will, in many instances, provide home addresses, landline, and cell phone numbers for *free*. Type in the person's name and a known hometown and then click on the view free details tab.

Fee based background checks are also available on a number of websites. You may want to reserve using those only for serious relationship prospects. Not everyone you cross paths with, is worth spending money to investigate their background. Most people you meet online will likely be screened out by you for a variety of reasons. You may not be physically attracted to them. You may not like their overall profile presentation or general outlook on life.

There are also sites like https://socialcatfish.com/, https://buzzhumble.com/, and https://albion-services.com/ which allow you to upload photos of a perspective match to see if they have other profiles using the same photos.

Create Folders

Keeping track of what you have been told by different dating prospects can sometimes become difficult especially when you are in contact with several people. When you decide someone is worth investing more time to get to know better, you may want to create a folder using their name in your email account. In this folder, you can paste information he or she provided you with on the online dating site portal. You may also want to add notes from any phone conversations you have had with them or while on dates if things ever progress that far. People who lie, often tend to forget what they have said. Maintaining a folder can quickly help you scan and compare details.

Signs Someone May be Catfishing You

They refuse to video chat with you after weeks of having established a good rapport. These days anyone can set up a Skype, Google Hangouts, Google Duo, FaceTime, or WhatsApp account.

Each and every time you plan to meet in person, a *major emergency* on their end prevents it from happening. Excuses such as their car broke down and their cell phone died so they were unable to contact you are given. Another common excuse is a loved one suddenly died. Their *emergency* causes you to empathize with them rather than being angry. No one has bad luck all the time.

Another red flag is anyone who has very few photos on their social media page and not many friends. If all of their photos look like *professional* model headshots, that is another clue.

It goes without saying, if someone you've never met asks you to send them money *for any reason;* odds are, you're not only being *catfished* but you're also a target of a scam!

Beware of anyone who professes their love for you in a very short amount of time. The catfish wants to create an emotional connection as soon as possible. One tactic is to shower you with compliments and talk about all the things they plan to do with you in the future. According to the catfish, it was *divine intervention* that brought you two together especially if they live abroad.

Broken English, very formal English, or several typos and misspellings from someone who claims to be a highly educated U.S. citizen with a professional career, is also a *red flag*.

Meet Me in My Dreams....

Sidestep the Long-Distance Trap

Inevitably, almost everyone who joins an online dating site has the experience of connecting with someone who is considered a long distance away. If you live in the LA area, they live in New York or if you live in Miami, they live in Chicago. Each of these areas has millions of citizens and yet the love of your life rarely seems to live across town from you.

Accidents and the Unforeseen

Ideally, most people would choose to be in a relationship with someone who lives in their same town or at the very least, same state. Not many people intentionally seek out someone to have a long-distance relationship with.

Many of these relationships come about by accident or through some unforeseen situation. Someone visits from out of town and they click with a native. They spend the majority of their time together. They may even have become sexually intimate. When the time comes for them to part ways, emotions run high and they decide to try and maintain their relationship.

Loving a Road Warrior

Too often women in particular will set out to marry a really successful man, without considering long-term, how much they will be left alone with the children. Let's face it, most presidents, CEOs, VPs, surgeons, lawyers, entertainers, military service personnel, top politicians, or territory sales people; are rarely going to be home for dinner at 6PM each evening. Generally speaking, the more successful one is, the more likely they have to travel or put in long hours.

It's not uncommon for resentment to set in or to hear their mate say, "I didn't get married to be alone!" Another issue that often arises concerns trust, along with emotional and physical needs. Cheating is much easier, if one is inclined to do so, when couples don't spend much time together. It's also much harder to "make up" after an argument in a long-distance relationship.

Some couples do get *used* to being apart. In one such instance, I am aware of a guy who completed his four years of duty in the navy on a submarine and when he returned home for good, his marriage ended. His wife had gotten use to her routines with the children and making all of the decisions while he was away. Although he had been home for vacations, it wasn't the same once he was *home for good*. Too much absence eroded their harmony as a family unit.

No Light at the End of the Tunnel

You must define what is making a long-distance relationship work. Do you mean it leads to a marriage? Is it just a certain amount of time as in a year, two years, or three years? One major error people make with LDRs, is confusing *calendar time* with *actual time together*. A couple that has been together one weekend per quarter will say they've been together for a year but in truth their *actual time together* would be eight days. Some of these couples become engaged or get married without truly knowing one another. There is no substitute for spending time with a person in order to get to know them well before marrying them. Eight days surly isn't enough!

An important part of a successful long-distance relationship, is making sure there is a clear-cut timeline of future events. If you are committed to each other, you must have a plan.

The vast majority of couples in long distance relationships have no timeline or plan for when they will be together permanently. Long distance relationships were meant to be *temporary*. The goal is to be with the person you love. When there is no *count down* towards the day when one person moves, it is likely one of you will eventually want to throw in the towel. It is imperative to schedule regular visits if possible. No amount of phone calls, emails, texts, Skype, or sporadic visits, can cement a relationship in the same way as being together regularly.

At some point, someone has to make a move. A long-distance relationship without "a light at the end of the tunnel" is likely to fail. It's the counting down of the months, weeks, and days until you are finally done with the inconvenience of being in a long-distance relationship that keeps it strong!

The only great reason for being in a long-distance relationship is the belief she or he might be "the one". If you're just passing time with someone for fun, you might as well do that locally.

You are so **amazing!** I wish I could find **someone** like you.

Dodge the Friend Zone

The evening was pleasant enough. The conversation flowed as well as the wine. Laughter was genuine, and you found yourself thinking just maybe she might be "the one". As your car approached her residence, you wonder - should you lean in for a kiss goodnight or wait to see if she will invite you in? Your heart pounds as you approach her door. She suddenly stops and turns towards you extending her hand. In your mind you swear you heard a voice saying:

You are about to enter another dimension. A dimension not only of sight and sound, but of mind. A journey into a wondrous land of imagination. Next stop, the Friend Zone!

Hidden Agendas

Just about everyone has had a crush on someone who either did not acknowledge our romantic interest in them or they told us early on, they were only interested in having a *platonic* friendship. However, we believed given time they would recognize us as being "the one".

Our first experience in the *friend zone* usually takes place while we are still in school. Maybe you were the smart sweet girl the star of the football team called upon to help him with his homework or you were the *nice guy* who was always available to lend the cute cheerleader a hand. Secretly, you desired a relationship with this person as they shared their dating frustrations with you. In many instances they solicited your advice on how they should deal with their love interest. Many of us never revealed we had a crush on our friend. We suffered in silence.

Awkward Moment

There are some people who will work up the nerve to make a move after spending weeks, months, or years around someone. Maybe they are returning from a fun night out or someone is crying on the other's shoulder. The person with the crush attempts to give a kiss and is soundly pushed away. A moment of silence ensues, followed by an apology from the kiss initiator. There is an instant realization that the friendship has forever been altered. The friendship becomes distant.

Another method used, is simply to blurt out one's feelings towards a friend. More often than not, this leads to a discussion about not wanting to mess up a great friendship. In other instances, the person with the crush is treated as though they betrayed their friend by harboring romantic feelings towards them. A woman might wonder if a man was befriending her simply to get into her pants. A man might wonder if a woman was secretly sabotaging his relationships with other women when he was asking her for relationship advice in dealing with his girlfriend.

Avoid the Zone

Once we are done with school and get out into the working-world, some of us repeat our high school days by having secret crushes on co-workers. The vast majority of us move onto pursuing dates with people we meet at various single scenes, nightclubs, online dating sites, or through people we know. Occasionally, there are people you will have one or two dates with and determine there is no chemistry and you never want to see them again. In other instances, you may meet a wonderful person whom you could see yourself being friends with.

It is important to remember, the reason you were asked out is because they saw you as a potential romantic partner. Once you conclude there is no romantic future, it is best to state so as soon as possible. It is not necessary to be rude about it. Simply let them know you feel it would be a waste of both your time to go out again. Never offer friendship as a *consolation prize* in order to let someone down easy. Being honest upfront, keeps you from having to play games such as hide and seek when they attempt to call you or pull a vanishing act, also known as *ghosting,* after pretending you had a wonderful time.

For those who are extending the friendship option, please be honest with yourself. The worst way to invest your time is hanging around someone with a *hidden agenda* of hoping to convert a friendship into a romantic relationship. When someone states they want to be your *friend* or says, "Let's be friends first and see where it goes." Or suggests taking things slow, what they are really saying is they do not see *you* as potentially being *the one*. They want to keep their options open. If they thought you were possibly *the one,* they would not risk leaving you on the "open market". After all, there is no such thing as being "exclusive friends".

Michael Bolton probably recorded the all-time classic *friend zone* song; "How Am I Supposed to Live Without You". Trust me, you do not want to find yourself singing these lyrics once your friend announces his or her engagement: *"How am I supposed to carry on when all I've been living for is gone. And how can I blame you, when I built my world around the hope that one day, we'd be so much more than friends."* It really sounds pathetic when you say that out loud.

It is far easier for a partner or spouse to become a best friend, than it is for a platonic best friend to become someone's lover, mate, or spouse. Naturally, there are some exceptions. Generally speaking, if you are in the *friend zone* it's because the other person didn't see *you* as date material.

Sometimes Sadness Leads to Passion and Sometimes it Doesn't

Linda had been trying to reach her friend Bob all weekend to no avail. Monday night, he finally answered his phone sounding very despondent.

Linda: I've been trying to reach you for a couple of days. What's the matter?

Bob: I just learned my father died.

Linda: I'm so sorry to hear that. I'm coming over.

About an hour later Linda arrives at Bob's apartment with Chinese takeout. They sit down to eat and Bob talks about the good times he had with his dad. He begins to sob and Linda takes him in her arms. Gently she kisses him, unbuttons his shirt, and opens his pants. Soon they are having passionate sex. The following day she reiterates they are still just friends and nothing more.

Two Years Later

Bob has been calling Linda and she hasn't answered her phone. He finally reaches her and she tells him her father died. An hour later Bob shows up at her door with take out from Chili's. They sit down to eat as Linda reminisces about her childhood and father. Bob comforts her with a hug and kisses her on the forehead. Slowly he begins to undo her blouse. She quickly pushes his hand away.

Linda: Stop it!

Bob: What did I do wrong?

Linda: I just told you my father died!

Bob: I know.

Linda: (Yelling) What makes you think I want to have sex?

Bob: (He mumbles) We did it when my daddy died.

Linda: Just go home!

Befuddled and confused, Bob puts on his jacket and goes home. Linda calls her girlfriend to tell her how unbelievably selfish and insensitive Bob was.

I suppose it is debatable whether or not a man can provide *sympathy sex* without appearing to be taking advantage of a situation. Some people believe only women can be selfless in that way.

Going From Online to Offline

In order to succeed with online dating, you have to be willing to establish an *offline* relationship with the person you have been corresponding with. There are some individuals who either fear meeting in person or they are completely content with being in an online emotional relationship. Once you sense this is the case with someone, you have little choice but to friend zone them. As Marvin Gaye and Tammi Terrell once sang: "Ain't Nothing Like the Real Thing."

Let the Good Times **Roll**

Relax and Have Fun!

Finally, you have met someone online you actually feel a great connection with and have decided to meet in person. For safety and privacy reasons it is probably best to make the first meeting a lunch or daytime activity date, whereby each person provides their own transportation.

Make sure you have told a friend or relative about your date plans and where you will be meeting. Some people go as far as having someone call them at a certain point during the date, to make sure everything is fine or the caller gives them an excuse to leave if things are not going well. Having your own transportation also makes it easier to cut a date short.

Dress Appropriately

The great thing about going on a daytime date is you can usually get away with wearing a nice pair of jeans, a nice blouse, or shirt. You don't have to stress out over what to wear. There is also no need to become a nervous wreck over your hair or other things related to your appearance.

As long as you both look like your profile photos and show up on time, the date should start off fine.

Lighten Up!

It's a date and not an interrogation. If you are feeling anxious, it is probably because you may have chosen to meet someone too soon. In my upcoming book on *first dates,* I will spend more time on how to go about building a rapport and prescreening before agreeing to meet someone.

The most important thing you can do is relax and be yourself. This will encourage the other person to do the same. Keep the conversations on lighthearted topics and remember to smile or laugh if you are indeed enjoying yourself. Pay attention to what is said or not said but do not obsess over it. You want them to know you are giving them your full attention.

Ideally, you have shared some *inside jokes* between yourselves in phone calls or text messages. Normally a first date consists of flattery, flirtation, and laughter over a meal or a cup of coffee.

The primary goal of a first date is to verify your chemistry offline is as good as it is online.

Leave Them Wanting More

More often than not, it is best to avoid having a marathon date the first time you meet someone. One way to ensure the date does not run into the evening or night, is by setting expectations early on that you have another obligation at a certain time. Two to three hours is generally long enough to give you an idea as to whether you want to go out with them again, unless you spent those hours in a movie theatre. If that is the case, you might want to extend the date after the matinee by grabbing a bite to eat or having a drink afterwards, in order to have a conversation.

Check Please

There has been an ongoing debate over who should pay for the first date. Traditionally men always paid for the dates. However, with the advent of the women's rights movement and a push for equality, some women insist on paying their own way, while others prefer to maintain the tradition of men paying. Some women also do not like feeling a sense of obligation or they believe men have *expectations* of them based upon the amount spent on a date.

The best approach is whomever initiates or invites someone to go out should be *prepared* to pay regardless of their gender. I have heard some women proclaim a *real man* always pays. Hypothetically, that would mean a woman could *suggest* going to Hawaii and if the man loved the idea in her mind, *he should pay* for airline tickets, hotels, transportation, meals and all activities! Something as extravagant as a trip, should be discussed with no assumptions made.

One of the reasons I suggest making the first date a lunch date or daytime activity is because it usually helps to keep expenses down. Lunch in a causal restaurant is less expensive than dinner.

A first date is about *getting to know someone* better and not about how much money is spent. Truth be told, the date activity, whatever it may be, is simply a backdrop. If you are with someone whom you have *no chemistry* with, dining in a five-star restaurant will *not* lead to a second date.

Another benefit to going to a casual dining spot is that the service is not designed to drag out a meal. The last thing anyone wants is to feel *stuck on a bad date* at the start of a seven-course meal!

Always Date and Never Hang Out

These days, the fear of rejection seems to be so intensified that many people do not want to put themselves out there. Instead of asking someone out on a date, they will invite them to *hang out*.

"There's this great band playing at the park on Saturday and a group of us are planning to go. I was thinking, if you're not doing anything, you might want to come *hang out*. It should be fun."

I cannot tell you how many times I have seen questions posted in dating forums where people are trying to "figure out" if the person is *romantically interested* in them after *hanging out*.

Being vague helps the person extending the invite to feel less pain in the event their idea is shot down. However, it's really nothing but their own internal head game. They know how *they* feel and their true motives. If you are romantically interested, ask them out on a date! Cowards end up wasting valuable time languishing around in the *friend zone*.

In a world with over seven billion people, rejection just means next!

"**Knowledge** isn't power until it **is applied**."
– Dale Carnegie

Parting Thoughts

Remember, online dating is only one of many potential ways to meet someone new, find a mate, or casually date. It is far too easy to rely on one method of meeting new people if you choose to become lazy. Overlooking invitations to attend parties, happy hours, going out dancing, or attending various professional networking events, can cause a delay in meeting someone special.

Being aware and receptive to how others are engaging with you, can lead to new opportunities. Many people are so focused during transactions, they are unaware they are being flirted with!

Paralysis of Analysis

If you are like many readers, you have probably read several dating and relationship books or articles in your life. My challenge to you is to actually take the information and tips provided in this book and implement them before moving on to the next book. At some point, you have to find out what works for you. The only way to know what works is by giving it an earnest try.

Online dating doesn't suck, too many people suck at online dating! My hope is after having read this book; you have become enlightened and find whatever you are looking for online or offline.

"Love isn't finding the perfect person. It's seeing an imperfect person perfectly." – Sam Keen

Best wishes,

Kevin Darné

Help is Only a Click Away…

Additional Resources

In the event you do implement the tips provided in *Avoid the Catfish!* and would like to gather more information regarding other aspects of dating and relationships, I highly recommend you consider reading My Cat Won't Bark! (A Relationship Epiphany). If you would like more direct assistance, you can also reach me through Fiverr.com under the username lovealert911.

If you'd like to be among the first to be notified of upcoming books and events, you may email us at info@lovealert911.com include your name and request to be added to our *inner circle*.

Conation Enterprises and its affiliate Lovealert911.com, will never sell or share your email address.

Printed in Great Britain
by Amazon